What the Heart Wants

Isabella Lim

BookLeaf
Publishing
India | USA | UK

Presentation by *BookLeaf Publishing*

Web: www.bookleafpub.com

E-mail: info@bookleafpub.com

ISBN: 9789363319011

First edition 2024

Love

I wish
For love that stays
The kind that holds you close
And wraps you in his arms and says
I'm here

Would We Be Friends?

Would we be friends
If I never reached out
If I stopped putting out energy
For you to respond to

Would we be friends
If I disappeared
Would you even notice
Do you think you would?

You see this friendship
Is one-sided
And I've been blinded
By trying and trying

But I've tried enough and so
I don't think we'd be friends

Birthday

Celebrate one day
Ignoring the in between
Which were just as mine

Meditate

Silence when I sit down
In the chaos of my day
Close my eyes and meditate
Thoughts wander every way
Mind is racing
And I'm chasing
Feelings that don't stay
I find my breath
And count to ten
Then everything's okay

Magnets

Like magnets, they glanced, danced, and swung
into motion

Would You Be Friends Again

Would you be friends again
Even if it's better we're not
Do you regret what you said
When you're stuck in your thoughts

Do you remember the good times we had
And the memories we made
Despite all your acting
Instead of leaving you stayed

And now I find myself wishing
For what we never had
Cause you lied so well to me
To leave me so sad

I Want You Back

I want you back
Despite myself
I despise myself

Waiting

Here I am waiting
How'd we end up here again
I thought this was over
I thought we weren't friends

Yet I run into you
Again and again
And you want to talk
To just disappear in the end

I'm tired of waiting
To hear your response
You drive me insane
You hold me in bonds

And I tell myself to let go
But I'm holding on tight
You've made me hope again
In the one who isn't right

Closer

Here we are again
Me drawn towards you
And you lost in the dark

What you say to me
Tugs straight on my heart
And I reach closer
Knowing it'll tear me apart

What Is This Power

What is this power
That ties us together
I know it's not love
Or anything better

Is it obsession
With what was the past
Or pure desperation
In what will not last

I cannot say
What connects you and I
But here I am hurting
Still saying I'll try

I Hate You

I hate you
I love you
And that's but one issue

You terrify me
With the feelings inside me
I'm tied to the stakes
And nothing is safe
From this bewildering emotion
And the echoing motion
Of powerlessness
In my chest

Dessert

He gave me a dessert for free
For a painting I thought was debris
Kindness in action
And spiced with compassion
Made someone a blessing to me

A Regular Student

A regular student
Thought I knew it
Going to class
Having a blast

But empty inside
And lonely at night
A regular student
Just going through it

Stressing

Are you stressing
Cause I'm messing
With my head
And all I've read
Doesn't help
With this lesson

Upside Down

Upside down
Inside out
Judging how
I'm freaking out

Obsessed

Why was I so obsessed with him
Calling him on every whim
Texting him to come with me

Now there's nothing that I feel
And I'm questioning what is real
Of the words he says to me

Give a hug
Say good luck
Don't give a fuck

Caramel

Days are sweet like caramel
Passing by in drizzled droves
Taste the honey in the air
Hold the moments to you close

Nerves

Nerves are buzzing
Head is rushing
On my way today
Perspirating
Suffocating
No one's on their way

Stop

Head is spinning
Thoughts are winning
Of giving up
And saying enough

Head is dizzy
Thoughts are fizzy
No more working
Time to stop

Breakdown

Hold it in so no one sees
But it's leaking out the seams
Tears start running down my face
With these feeling I can't erase

Praying that the time will end
They're still talking so I blend
All the background noise away
But cries still slip out anyway

See their faces talking back
About the things that I so lack
Running down the hall to cry
And I'm questioning the reason why

Bawling and the tears won't stop
Wondering if I can flop
Down onto this bathroom floor
And say I can't do it no more

Leaves

Freshly fading leaves
Fall apart around my friend
As I turn away